Sacrifice

T0303641

Breakthroughs in Mimetic Theory

Edited by William A. Johnsen

Sacrifice
René Girard

Translated by Matthew Pattillo and David Dawson

Michigan State University Press

East Lansing

Sacrifice is a series of lectures given in 2002 at the National Library of France.

Copyright © 2011 by René Girard

Le sacrifice copyright © 2003 Bibliothèque Nationale of Paris

This series is supported by Imitatio, a project of the Thiel Foundation.

♾ The paper used in this publication meets the minimum requirements of ANSI/NISO Z39.48-1992 (R 1997) (Permanence of Paper).

Michigan State University Press
East Lansing, Michigan 48823-5245

Printed and bound in the United States of America.

        3   4   5   6   7   8   9   10

Library of Congress Cataloging-in-Publication Data

Girard, René, 1923–
  [Sacrifice. English]
  Sacrifice / René Girard ; translated by Matthew Pattillo and David Dawson.
    p. cm. — (Breakthroughs in mimetic theory)
  Translation of: Le sacrifice. Bibliothèque nationale de France : Diffusion Seuil, c2003.
  Includes bibliographical references.
  ISBN 978-0-87013-992-5 (pbk. : alk. paper)
  1. Sacrifice—Hinduism—History of doctrines. 2. Brahmanas—Criticism, interpretation, etc. 3. Sacrifice in the Bible. I. Title.
  BL1236.76.S23G4713 2011
  203'.42—dc22

                                   2011002589

Cover and book design by Erin Kirk New

Cover art © Ali Mazraie Shadi

 Michigan State University Press is a member of the Green Press Initiative and is committed to developing and encouraging ecologically responsible publishing practices. For more information about the Green Press Initiative and the use of recycled paper in book publishing, please visit www.greenpressinitiative.org.

Visit Michigan State University Press on the World Wide Web at:
www.msupress.msu.edu

In memoriam Sylvain Lévi

Contents

Preface

Anthropological thought long saw blood sacrifice as a kind of enigma, one it endeavored to solve, but without success. It then told itself that sacrifice in general, sacrifice as such, perhaps does not exist. The hypothesis of a conceptual illusion is legitimate as a hypothesis, but during the second half of the twentieth century it hardened into a dogma all the more intolerant for believing itself triumphant over Western intolerance, over our intellectual imperialism.

Under the sway of this dogma, the majority of researchers have rejected the mimetic theory which reaffirms the enigmatic nature of sacrifice and sees its universality as rooted in the mimetic violence of all archaic groups, in the unanimous lynching of real victims—something produced spontaneously in disturbed communities, where it serves to restore peace.

Communities deliberately reproduce these phenomena in their sacrificial rites, hoping in this way to protect themselves from their own violence by diverting it onto expendable victims, human or animal, whose deaths will not cause violence to rebound because no one will bother to avenge them. To illustrate mimetic theory, I will interrogate the most powerful religious reflections on sacrifice, those of Vedic India, collected in the vertiginous Brahmanas. Between the conceptions of the Brahmins and my theory the coincidences are too numerous and striking to be accidental. Alongside the convergences, to be sure, there are divergences but, far from contradicting mimetic theory, they correspond to the minimum of illusion without which sacrifice becomes impossible. For sacrifice to be possible, the original victim must first be held responsible for the mimetic disorder and then, through the mediation of unanimous violence, for the return to order. It is as though we are dealing with a god who, after terrorizing the community, takes pity on it and teaches it to sacrifice.

One finds everywhere in the Bible collective violence similar to that which generates sacrifice, but instead of attributing responsibility for the violence to the victims—who are only conciliators in appearance, by virtue of the transference carried out against them at the expense of the truth—the Bible and the Gospels attribute it to its true perpetrators, the persecutors of the single victim. Instead of elaborating myths, consequently, the Bible and the Gospels tell the truth.

Once exposed, as it is in the Bible and the Gospels, the mechanism of victimization can no longer function as the model for would be sacrificers. If the term *sacrifice* is used for the death of Jesus, it is in a sense absolutely contrary to the archaic sense. Jesus consents to die in order to reveal the lie of blood sacrifices and to render them henceforth impossible. The Christian notion of redemption must be interpreted on the basis of this reversal.

One thus finds in the Bible and the Gospels the explanation of the sacrificial process. When John the Baptist refers to Jesus as "the Lamb of God," or when Jesus refers to himself as "the stone rejected by the builders, who becomes the cornerstone," the sacrificial process appears and loses its efficacy. The revelation and repudiation of sacrifice go hand in hand, and all of this is found, up to a certain point, in the Vedanta and in the Buddhist refusal of sacrifices.

By recognizing that the Vedic tradition can also lead to a revelation that discredits sacrifice, mimetic theory locates within sacrifice itself a paradoxical power of quiet reflection that leads, in the long run, to the eclipse of this violent institution that is nevertheless fundamental for the development of humanity. Far from unduly privileging the Western tradition and awarding it a monopoly on the knowledge and repudiation of blood sacrifice, mimetic analysis recognizes the comparable but never truly identical traits in the Indian tradition. Even if we remain unable to fully disentangle the ties that unite and separate these two traditions, we will appreciate a little better their richness and complexity.

—René Girard

1

Sacrifice in the Vedic Tradition

Mimetic Rivalry and Sacrifice in the Brahmanas

After some hesitation, at the end of the nineteenth and beginning of the twentieth century anthropology turned resolutely to the study of individual cultures. Researchers began to take very seriously the differences between cultures, but without renouncing the great theoretical questions that presuppose the unity of man. They believed that beyond the archaic cults, each different from the others, there was the enigma of religion as such and that its solution must be imminent.

Everyone was more or less agreed that blood sacrifice lay at the heart of this enigma. Beyond carefully descriptive essays such as Hubert and Mauss's *Essay on the Nature and Function of Sacrifice*,[1] ambitious researchers dreamed of working out a definitive theory that would at last explain why, in the most diverse cultures, with the exception of the Christian and the modern world which issues from it, men have always immolated victims to their divinities.

After a century of aborted attempts, in the middle of the twentieth century anthropologists began to wonder, quite legitimately, whether they were doomed to failure by a premise implicit in their efforts: the unity of religion, which presupposes that of human culture. They wondered whether anthropology had not been the victim of "Western ethnocentrism."

Nothing is more praiseworthy than mistrust of ethnocentrism. How could it fail to threaten us, when all modern anthropological concepts come from the West, including that of ethnocentrism—a charge that is brandished by the West alone, and against itself exclusively?

Mistrust of ethnocentrism is more than legitimate; it is indispensable, and yet we must not make of it the prehistoric bludgeon that false progressivism and false radicalism made of it in the second half of the twentieth century. The notion of ethnocentrism was made to serve a poorly disguised anti-intellectualism that reduced to silence the most legitimate anthropological curiosity. For several years the frenzy of "deconstruction" and demolition sustained an intense excitement in research that today has collapsed, killed by its own success.

It is not excessive ambition that threatens us now, but bureaucratization and provincialization as research is more and more limited to the local and the particular. Once the great questions are discredited, for want of intellectual stimulation anthropology languishes. Still quite lively in the era of Durkheim and the early Lévi-Strauss, the discipline has since tended to settle into a rather disappointing academic routine.

If it were clear that the celebrated "differences" are alone real, that they override resemblances and identities in every case, we would gladly resign ourselves to this situation. But the dogmatic nihilism of the last quarter century is little more than an avant-garde slogan doubling as a flagrant logical absurdity. Research is brought to heel with the intimidation "post-colonialist," and this cannot last forever.

No, sacrifice cannot be defined primarily as a "discourse." No, Saussurian analysis cannot settle its score with religion. A science begins by flouting common sense at its own peril. We must return to the modest realism of fledgling disciplines.

We must rekindle the curiosity that is the true impetus of anthropology, which is more and more intimidated by the snobbery of the void. We are the first great civilization to completely rid ourselves of sacrifice. The intense curiosity this institution inspires in us is inseparable from our singularity in this respect; it is not thereby disqualified.

Classical anthropology asked the right questions. If the answers failed to come, it is not necessarily because they do not exist; it might be because we refuse to seek them where they may be found. Far from exhausting the possibilities of inquiry, anthropology, in its research on sacrifice, has always conjured away the most obviously relevant fact: *violence*.

There exists a very old and powerful taboo against religious violence. Rather than liberating us from it, radical avant-gardism only reinforces it by denouncing as obviously tendentious and "reactionary" the refusal to conjure away the violence of archaic religion. Realistic exploration is condemned as an attempt to denigrate archaic cultures that in reality have long ceased to exist.

To combat the taboo surrounding religious violence, we must begin by properly locating it. To do this, we should inquire first of that philosopher who, because he vigorously defended this taboo, was obliged to formulate it explicitly at the risk of undermining it. Any taboo too clearly articulated is, for that very reason, threatened.

Plato condemns all literary representations of religious violence. He excludes from his perfect city those artists who make what he considers an obscene and scandalous display of this violence, namely Homer and the tragic poets. What is it the philosopher dreads? Quite simply, a decomposition of religion that is liable to pervade society as a whole.

When we attentively examine archaic religions, we can see that, far from being a Platonic innovation, the concern with dissimulating or minimizing violence is already present at the center of ritual sacrifice. It belongs to the religious itself. Vedic sacrifice, for example, tries hard to minimize its own violence. The rites are organized so as to render the murder of victims as inconspicuous as possible.

Vedic India had no temples and so, before performing a sacrifice, priests would trace the boundaries of a site officially consecrated to this purpose, but *it was outside of these boundaries that the immolation was performed.* To better conceal the act and avoid the spectacle of bloodshed, they surreptitiously strangled the victim instead of cutting his throat, as was once done.

This ambiguous attitude is common. Many sacrificial systems make a point of minimizing their own violence, excusing it, sometimes even apologizing to victims before immolating them. Joseph de Maistre makes much of these maneuvers in his celebrated "Traité sur les sacrifices,"[2] but they are too theatrical, it seems to me, to truly mean what they purport to mean.

By acting as they do, scrupulous sacrificers repeatedly call attention to the violence they pretend to conceal. They suggest to us the true nature of sacrifice, which is really always a kind of murder. It has less to do with renouncing violence—sacrifice hardly renounces that—than with emphasizing its transgressive power. Sacrifice is simultaneously a murder and a most holy act. Sacrifice is divided against itself.[3]

It is undoubtedly no coincidence that, in Vedic India once again, the genuinely violent sacrifices dispense with the charade of nonviolence. The Great Sacrifice of the Horse, for example, comprises as a rule, among other victims, the immolation of a human being. There is no reason to doubt that it took place. This human sacrifice is, however, mentioned casually, as if it were nothing. On the other hand, the charade of feigned violence is played up during rites that are foreign to any real violence, as in the case of soma.

The Sacrifice of Soma

Soma is a plant that grew wild on the Himalayan slopes. Sacrificers derived from it a potion they considered divine, probably for its hallucinogenic properties. There is no certainty on this point because no one is able to identify the plant hiding behind the term *soma*. All we know is that use of the potion derived from it was made a part of sacrificial rites.

Freshly cut stems were pressed between stones to obtain the draught. This operation was itself an important sacrificial rite, for it was likened to the most reprehensible murder, that of a Brahmin, a member of the highest caste, to which gods like Soma also belonged.

When the Vedic commentators consider sacrifice, the less reason there is to be terrified, the more terrified they pretend to be. This leads us to wonder whether sacrifice does not seek to provoke the shock of extreme violence that actors and spectators commonly experience in the theater. The more insignificant the victim, the lower it is situated in the scale of being, the more difficult that shock is to achieve.

There exists a hierarchy of sacrificial victims which is completely universal and, strangely enough, each of us can attest to it because it resides deep within us and requires no explanation: humans are at the top, animals are in the middle, and plant life on the bottom. It is doubtless to obtain the optimum effect—neither too strong nor too weak—that the Brahmanas "dramatize" to the limit the "sacrifice" of soma and play down that of the human.

What replaces sacrificial rites in our day, insofar as they can be effectively replaced, is violent spectacle. Depending on the dose, the calming effect can be transformed into a violent thrill, an insalubrious incitement. Everything depends here on a modulation similar to that which the Brahmanas seek to achieve, by minimizing the violence of rites which, "objectively," contain too much of it, and by exaggerating the violence of rites that contain too little. During times of upheaval, the system breaks down and violence mounts in the spectacles at the same pace as in the street. This tendency inspired in the sages an anxiety like that of Plato reading Homer.

The Brahmanas

We know the Indian sacrifice called Vedic thanks to the Vedas, sacred books that are even today universally venerated. The word *veda* means "knowledge," "science." What is the object of Vedic science? Sacrifice, naturally, which is the true unifying principle of this religion. The Vedic scriptures are a world little known in the West, with the very limited exception of the Rig Veda, the Veda of strophes and hymns belonging to the first stratum of this great collection. It is the best known of all the Vedic books, in India as in the West. The texts cited in these lectures come neither from the Rig Veda nor from the first stratum of the Vedas but from the second, comprising vast compilations of rituals and commentaries on sacrifice: the Brahmanas.

Is it perhaps imprudent on my part to interpret difficult, sometimes bewildering texts whose language is unknown to me? What gives me the audacity is the existence of a book that is a kind of selective anthology of the Brahmanas with many citations translated into French, *La Doctrine du sacrifice dans les Brahmanas* by Sylvain Lévi.[4] It is not the original Sanskrit text that I interpret, but Sylvain Lévi's book.

It dates to an era (1898) when the most famous Indianists of Europe and America not only scorned the Brahmanas but heaped insults on them. They did not hesitate to treat their authors as feebleminded, as saboteurs of their own culture.[5] Lévi believes, on the contrary, in the coherence of these books and that is why he strives to make them accessible to simple amateurs like myself.

In Lévi's time, the Brahmanas had such a bad reputation that his book went largely unremarked. When Presses Universitaires de France reprinted it in 1966 things had scarcely changed, to judge from Louis Renou's preface. This eminent Indianist confessed that the Brahmanas' ultimate incoherence remained more plausible, in his eyes, than the coherence postulated by Sylvain Lévi.

I take the side of Sylvain Lévi in this debate. I think that the coherence of the Brahmanas is real, and that it is the same, in the last analysis, as that of all archaic sacrificial systems, though here it takes an original form because it is more developed, more intellectualized than elsewhere, and because the Brahmanas transcend themselves, as we shall see, in some later texts that radically criticize sacrifice.

Though not the same as Sylvain Lévi's, my interpretation of the Brahmanas—through his book—vindicates his confidence in the intellectual power of the great Vedic texts. It is therefore to the memory of this researcher that I dedicate the present work, as a token of admiration and gratitude.

The Rivalries of the Devas and the Asuras

What immediately disconcerts the modern reader when faced with the Brahmanas are the countless little narratives—never identical but always fairly similar, as far as I am able to judge—that are strewn throughout these works. They all deal with the same theme: the intense rivalry, ever renewed, between the Devas and the Asuras, that is, between gods and demons.

For lack of time, I shall not be able to say all I would like, nor fully defend what I shall say, and for this I apologize. To begin, I shall observe that, despite the absence of human beings from these little dramas, they have as much to do with humankind as with gods and demons. In this world humans, like the gods and demons, are created by sacrifice itself, which becomes a creator in the figure of Prajâpati, the greatest of all the gods. All Prajâpati's intelligent creatures are devoted to rivalries and therefore to sacrifice, for only sacrifice, as we shall see, is able to quell their rivalries.

To study these little dramas carefully we would require more numerous citations than those placed at our disposal by Sylvain Lévi, who was not, of course, able to translate them all. But if the samples he has chosen are representative, and I believe they must be, they reveal a number of essential things about Vedic sacrifice.

First, a leading example of these narratives:

The Devas and the Asuras born of Prajâpati were in contention [for the world]. Now the world was wavering like a lotus petal in the wind; it went now to the Devas, now to the Asuras. As it drew close to the Gods, they said: Come, let us consolidate this world, to make of it a place of rest; once it is strengthened and stable, let us establish there the fires [of sacrifice]. [Then let us offer a sacrifice] and let us prevent our rivals from having a share. . . . They [offered a sacrifice] and kept their rivals from having a share.[6]

This world that oscillates like a lotus petal blown by the wind is not as deplorable as the nineteenth-century scholars claim; it is even rather pretty, is it not? But the authors of these books care little, apparently, about the aesthetic effect produced by their writings. What interests them are the rivalries, the most consistent feature of which is their obstinacy, both camps refusing any compromise.

Where does this intransigence come from? At first glance it seems to be the importance of what is at stake, the object of the rivalry, often something priceless, as in the present case. There is always an object that both the gods and demons hope to possess exclusively. It is often something as enormous, splendid, fantastic as the imagined antagonists themselves. Here it is the world; elsewhere it will be the sun, the moon, and so on. The gods and demons contend for all of creation.

The object is often *impossible to divide,* and for good reason, for what is at stake is in truth an abstraction rather than a real, material object. It is Vâc, for example, the Voice, or rather language that the Devas and the Asuras dispute; or it is the Year, signifying time. In a fair number of cases, however, the gods and demons dispute goods that appear easily divided, those that men, especially in Vedic India, bitterly dispute—cattle, for example. Actually here, too, division is impossible, for it is not a question of a few or even a great number of cattle but of cattle as such, the abstract idea of cattle.

It is never the same object twice in a row. Indeed, in each episode the Devas prevail over the Asuras thanks to a sacrifice, one they perform better than their rivals, and this ritual victory ensures their ownership of the disputed object. The further we go, the better we understand that the objects are of little importance. They are but pretexts for rivalry. Their acquisition by the gods, who are always victorious, means simply that the gods are advancing steadily in their patient march toward immortality and divinity in the classical sense, a status they did not at first possess. The demons, on the other hand, sink further and further into the demonic.

If the object is secondary, what is essential to these rivalries? Is it the bellicose temperament of the rivals, their ill humor? It is clear that neither the Devas nor the Asuras love peace. The gods—at least in the texts translated by Lévi—are even more grasping and aggressive than the demons. Together, they manage to revive their rivalry even under circumstances most favorable to its extinction.

The case of the moon illustrates this clearly. It is an object that the gods and demons desire simultaneously. Unlike so many other objects, the moon, at least in Vedic astronomy, is eminently divisible. Every month, it divides itself into a waning moon and a waxing moon. To avoid a new rivalry, I suppose, Prajâpati has decided to allot the first to the Devas, the second to the Asuras. One could not imagine a more equitable solution, but the Devas will not hear of it:

The gods had a desire: how may we capture the share of the Asuras? They went worshiping and grieving [practicing competitive asceticism]. They saw the rites of the new moon and the full moon, they celebrated them, and they won the share that belonged to the Asuras.[7]

The gods disobey their creator and principal protector. Far from being punished, they are rewarded because they "see" the appropriate rites and perform them flawlessly. As always, the rivalry leads to sacrifice and the sacrifice, as always, resolves the quarrel in favor of the Devas, who make off with the entire moon right under Prajâpati's nose.

Rivalry and Imitation

To understand just how crucial rivalry is to these narratives, we should note, with Sylvain Lévi, the rigor and consistency of the terms designating it.[8] In a first group of volumes, the sacred word is *spardh,* which means "rivalry"; in a second group it is *samyat,* which instead means "conflict." These terms clearly have a technical sense. These are the terms that professors and students (*brahmacarin*) employ in their seminars on sacrifice.

What interests me in these rivalries is the mimicry that obviously provokes them and that, becoming reciprocal, forces their escalation. To find the source of these rivalries, we must examine the beginning of each episode, for it is always the same: the two groups are separated but they never cease observing one another; as soon as one of the two reaches for an object, the second anxiously follows suit; soon there are two desires in place of one, two desires bound to collide since they have the same object. Everywhere, imitation is the engine of rivalry.

This imitation accounts for all the symmetries, all the reciprocities that mark our narratives *before* the intervention of sacrifice, and sacrifice produces a decisive difference, always in favor of the gods. The demons are shown to be almost as clever as the gods, almost as precise in ritual practice, but not quite; this is the sole reason for their repeated descent into the demonic and for the gods' ascension toward the divine.

If the rivalries always begin again after their sacrificial conclusion, it is not because the conflict is poorly extinguished, but because there are always new objects kindling new desires and these new desires kindle new rivalries, which are cooled each time by new sacrificial interventions. These interventions may long go undecided, but in the end they are always decided in favor of the gods.

This perpetual imitation of the desire of the other that one finds everywhere in the Brahmanas is not reserved to the gods and demons alone. It also occurs among humans. Imitation is at work among all Prajâpati's intelligent creatures—humans, gods, and demons. It is inseparable, by all accounts, from the extreme violence of the relations between them, those who must resort to sacrifice again and again to resolve conflicts and to differentiate themselves from one another.

Over the course of more than forty years, I have developed a conception of desire closer to that of the Brahmanas than to current Western ideas. I call it mimetic desire, and for those who are unacquainted with it, I shall give a brief summary.

Unlike basic appetites, desire is a social phenomenon that originates in an already existing desire, that of the majority, for example, or that of an individual whom we take as a *model* without even noticing it, because we admire him, because everyone admires him. Subjective experience contradicts the truth of desire. The more intense the desire, the more it seems to be ours and ours alone. But this experience is deceptive. It is not by chance that the most intense desire is always the most frustrated. The proof is that, as soon as it ceases to be frustrated, its intensity diminishes. No one fans my desire as effectively as the one who inspires it by desiring for himself, diabolically, or so it seems, an object I believe I desire independently of his influence. The more mimetic a desire is, the more intense it becomes. The intensity of desire persuades us of its "authenticity," when in reality the model is all-powerful. The modern world "demystifies" and "deconstructs" all secondary illusions, but only to reinforce the fundamental illusion of desire, which does not elude the Brahmanas.

When we moderns, at least in the West, consider desire in general and especially our own desire, we invariably conclude that we have chosen it ourselves, with no interference from without. We side with those who situate desire in the

Self, the subject, the Ego, in the celebrated "depths of subjectivity," which are, of course, "unfathomable."

Our world, especially scholars in the humanities, ever faithful to the optimism of the Enlightenment, believes in the spontaneity of desire. This, in my opinion, is the principal reason for the hostility of the nineteenth-century Indianists toward the Brahmanas, and of other academic disciplines toward mimetic theory.

This theory sees, by contrast, what the Brahmanas also see. If rivalry is always present between the Devas and the Asuras, it is because mimetic desire is equally present. Many indications confirm that everything in the Brahmanas is organized by the principle of mimetic desire. One of the most conspicuous aspects of this conformity is the loss of differentiation, the blurring of the distinction between gods and demons in the course of their rivalries. Nothing can be said of one that must not also be said of the other. Violent reciprocity makes them exact copies of each other, like the enemy twins who abound in archaic myths.

In founding myths, the theme of enemy twins often stands for the undifferentiating reciprocity of mimesis. In the Brahmanas the question of twins is posed apropos of the Devas and the Asuras, but it is never resolved. It is presented as undecidable. And that, it seems to me, is a radical version of mythic undifferentiation. To call the gods and demons twins would be to make them too nearly identical, and this is what the Brahmanas refuse to do. The gods and the demons are *not quite* twins. An undecidable case of twins is even more insurmountable than the explicit case of twins:

> Two higher orders of creatures emanated from Prajâpati: the Devas and the Asuras. The birthright is undecided between the two groups; primogeniture is assigned now to one, now to the other.[9]

Only one thing in our little dramas is more important than the rivalries—the sacrifice that concludes them. The fact that the rivalries always begin again, after each sacrificial conclusion, does not mean that these endings are temporary, or provisional. The proof that they are not is that the gods decisively acquire the disputed object. The rivalries always begin again, but each time over a new object and a new desire. The little dramas of the Brahmanas are, in this sense, like a stairway that ascends for the gods, a stairway that descends for the demons.

The Coming of Sacrifice

Though it be more or less delayed, the sacrificial conclusion is inevitable. It can occur immediately, with the first sacrifice, or it may occur later, at the end of a double series of sacrifices, those of the gods and those of the demons. Sometimes it is the gods who take the initiative to sacrifice, sometimes the demons. Sometimes too it is Prajâpati: the sacrifice god himself who "sees" the first sacrifice, and his intervention is the most decisive. If rivalries are sufficiently aggravated, they are capable of generating—in fact they alone generate—not the ritual sacrifice directly, of course, but its origin, the founding murder, the model of ritual sacrifice. Sacrifice is not, in principle, a human invention.

Between the rivalries and sacrifice there exists an affinity that is never denied. I see proof of it in the fact that, as soon as a sacrifice is offered, it does not matter where, it does not matter by whom, the gods rush in to contend for it. Each of them hopes the sacrifice will be offered to him alone and that the other gods will be excluded. Indeed, even in the absence of the demons, among the gods alone, whenever it is a question of sacrifice, rivalries ignite:

> [. . .] all these gods arrive with rival claims [. . .]. All the divinities surround the priest at the moment when he goes to make the offering: "It is for me that he is making it!"—"It is for me!"[10]

Only the mechanism of victimization and the conditions that trigger its release are able to account for the close but complex relationship between the rivalry and sacrifice, which expel each other reciprocally yet remain inseparable.

The Brahmanas are more perceptive than our human sciences, and see the mimetic nature of desire. If rivalries abound in these works, it is because they abound in our world and because they always accompany sacrifice. The survival of communities everywhere would be under constant threat if sacrifice did not intervene, sometimes on its own initiative, to make an end of rivalry.

When mimetic relationships begin to deteriorate, we need not despair; on the contrary, it is not always necessary that violence be renounced. Perhaps it is even advisable that the rivalries be given time to worsen, the better to facilitate sacrifice. Cleverness counts for as much as piety in these matters. The best sacrificers are those most artful at negotiating the dangers of our world.

The Brahmins' confidence in sacrifice is absolute. They recommend sacrifice instead of renunciation, but not to just anyone. It is to the *ksatryas,* the princely caste, the warrior aristocracy who were to some extent the Brahmins' clients in the matter of sacrifice. The Brahmins count on sacrifice to resolve every problem in favor of the princes they serve.

Far from stigmatizing the competitive avidity of the gods, the Brahmanas encourage it. To settle conflicts, they always suggest sacrifice rather than moderation and nonviolence. The authors here clearly have in mind only the class of princes and the warrior aristocrats, the *ksatryas,* for they alone have the means to offer sacrifices. Instead of preaching moderation and nonviolence, the Brahmanas recommend sacrifice, the business that ensures their survival. They advertise for sacrifice.

This confidence in sacrifice is not absurd in principle, even if in the long run, inevitably, it becomes so. The Brahmins speak of sacrifice as if it were a purely human technique, as if they knew that the power of peace and order inhabiting it, real as it is, depends less on a properly religious transcendence than on something unknown, unknown except for the conditions that trigger its release. It is essential, therefore, to scrupulously respect these conditions; they are in principle one with the ritual regulations. Here again the convergence with mimetic theory is astonishing. I will now summarize the perspective of mimetic theory on this original phenomenon and its reproduction in ritual.

The Single Victim Mechanism

When mimetic rivalries cross a certain threshold of intensity, the rivals forget, misplace, or destroy the disputed objects and lay hold of one another directly. Hatred of the rival then prevails over desire for the object. It is the moment when all seems lost, and in many cases, perhaps, this loss is final. But in other cases everything is saved, as we have seen, by sacrifice. How, specifically, does this salvation come about?

As long as the rivals contend for objects, they are unable to get along. Once the objects are destroyed, pushed aside, or forgotten, the rivals come face to face and all seems lost because the violence redoubles, but, on the contrary, everything is saved. Paradoxically, what desire for the same object can never accomplish—reconciliation of the adversaries—hatred for a common enemy does. Two, then three, then four antagonists form an alliance against a fifth and, little by little, mimeticism mounts, to the ruin of one antagonist more or less arbitrarily selected. In the end, the entire system tips over into unanimity against a single adversary, a scapegoat chosen by mimeticism itself.

The mounting confusion, the loss of differentiation, polarizes an entire community against a single individual, a supreme enemy who all at once appears solely responsible for the catastrophe and is promptly lynched. The community finds itself suddenly deprived of the enemy and tranquility is restored. At first universally reviled, the victim soon becomes a savior by reason of his reconciling power.

The miracle of sacrifice is the formidable "economy" of violence that it realizes. It directs against a single victim the violence that, a moment before, menaced the entire community. This liberation appears all the more miraculous for intervening in extremis, at the very moment when all seems lost.

Each time a community is saved by the scapegoat mechanism it rejoices, but it is soon alarmed to find that the effects of the founding murder are temporary, and that it risks falling back into rivalries it has only just managed to escape.

Driven by fear, all human communities behave in a similar fashion. They attempt to reproduce the miracle that has saved them by immolating a new victim in place of the first, in the hope that the same cause will produce the same effects. And this is what happens wherever human communities survive and flourish. The power to make peace is weakened little by little but, for a period of time, whenever a new victim is immolated in conformity with the initial model, the violence dies down. Humanity's first cultural initiative is the imitation of the founding murder, which is one with the invention of *ritual sacrifice*.

In many archaic societies, the great sacrifices begin with a simulacrum of crisis, a staged disordering of the community. No anthropologist has ever really understood why. The strategists of sacrifice saw clearly in mimetic rivalries a factor favorable to the activation of the reconciling mechanism, and they deliberately cultivated them in preparation for sacrifice, to facilitate the polarization of a single victim. The mimetic rivalries of the Brahmanas are a literary representation of the same idea.

Sacrificial rites quite probably began as what Frazer calls "scapegoat rites," for they are all copies of the same spontaneous phenomena and are always easily recognizable. All human communities developed sacrificial systems in times past, each of them different from the others, to be sure, for copies of models are never identical although they remain essentially alike. In the Brahmanas, the sacrifices offered by Prajâpati symbolize, perhaps, the founding phenomenon itself. The sacrifices offered by the gods and demons symbolize the sacrificial rituals.

The Brahmanas are especially perceptive about the genesis of religion in that they exalt the sacrificial process itself above its victims. Most sacrificial systems do the reverse. In the Brahmanas the gods are not, however, suppressed and the greatest of them all becomes, as I have said, sacrifice itself: Prajâpati.

2
The Founding Myths of Vedic Sacrifice

In my first lecture, I spoke of the nearly obligatory prelude to sacrifice—the rivalries of the gods and demons in the Brahmanas, the great Vedic commentaries on sacrifice. These rivalries are the reciprocal imitations of desire. They are therefore mimetic in the sense given this term by mimetic theory and so, at the moment of paroxysm, these rivalries spontaneously engender the sacrifice that interrupts them.

What the reason for this sudden change is, the Brahmanas do not say. Mimetic theory, following its scientific inspiration, insists the change must be a purely natural phenomenon released during the paroxysm of violent rivalries for natural and identifiable reasons, a phenomenon largely ignored by anthropologists and sociologists. I have shown that mimeticism must suddenly change direction and seize a single victim, who is obviously irrelevant but who is nevertheless promptly lynched by the unanimous community. I call this the founding murder, or single victim mechanism. For the price of one violent act, limited to a single victim, it reconciles the community against and finally around this same victim. In the end the victim is seen as almost too good to be true. He is taken for a savior. Simultaneously violent and peaceful, malevolent and benevolent, he is divinized in the sense of the archaic sacred.

Incessant rivalry is at once a social pathology that is potentially lethal to human communities and a condition favorable to the spontaneous release of the only phenomenon likely to put an end to it, which we may call a scapegoat phenomenon. But perhaps I would do better to give up this expression for it; I realize now that it causes misunderstandings.[11] Every human community realizes quickly, inevitably, that the beneficial effects of the founding murder do not last forever and they attempt to renew them by imitating the first murder, immolating new victims chosen deliberately for this role. The invention of ritual sacrifice must be the first properly human initiative, the point of departure for religious culture, which is to say, the point of departure for human culture itself.

Sacrifice is not then merely an instrument of peace; it sets in motion a process of repetition that engenders, no doubt very gradually, what we call our social and political institutions. The more sacrifices are repeated, the more they tend to become what we call funerals, marriages, rites of passage, initiations of all sorts, and likewise royalty—political power is always suffused with the sacred—all the institutions, in short, of our culture.

The benefits that humanity derives from sacrifices are therefore real, and only this reality can account for the attachment of sacrificial peoples to them. Without sacrifices, humanity would have succumbed not once but a thousand times over to the destructive power of its own violence during the major portion of its history, and especially during its immense prehistory. Just as mimetic crises and their resolutions never unfold in exactly the same fashion, so too sacrifices are never exactly the same in different societies; nevertheless they always look enough alike to be recognizable as sacrifices. Recent attempts to deny the universality of this institution are plainly contrary to common sense and are sterilizing to the study of religion.

Human culture is fundamentally and originally religious rather than secondarily and supplementally. The most formidable ethnocentrism does not minimize the celebrated differences between cultures, which no one would think to do in our day, but, on the contrary, exaggerates them so as better to ignore the universal role of religion, not only in the survival of humanity but in the social organization that has slowly emerged from sacrificial rites and that the Brahmanas interpret precisely in terms of difference.

My relative justification of archaic religion—my acknowledgement of its social function—does not warrant the claim of some that I exempt myself from the community of "serious" researchers, that I do not even deserve to be refuted because my thought is a product of religious inspiration and blatantly transgresses scientific rationality. It suffices to read my books with a minimum of attention to prove the falsity of this accusation. Mimetic theory renders an account of sacrifice and archaic religion in terms of a purely natural force, human hypermimeticism. Because it exacerbates rivalries, this hypermimeticism destroys the dominance patterns in animal societies, but it replaces them, in the paroxysm of violence it releases, with another natural restraint: the mechanism of victimization, the founding murder that produces ritual sacrifice in its turn. In this genesis, there is not the slightest recourse to transcendence or to anything "irrational."

The religious belief common to all archaic societies, including the Vedic, consists in thinking that the "miracle" of sacrifice, the minimal character of its violence, is too good to be true and so incomprehensible that it seems beyond natural explanation. They appeal therefore to an absolute, properly transcendental power beyond the human. Archaic thought never overcomes this religious illusion, even in the most perspicacious systems—the Vedic, for example—but this illusion coexists in the Vedic scriptures with a knowledge of the sacrificial function far superior to all the pseudo-demystifications that traditional modern accounts propose to us.

The religious reflection of the Vedic world is entirely centered on sacrifice. It shows an exceptional perspicacity by insisting on the mimetic rivalries that precede and engender this mysterious institution. Prior to the Brahmanas, attention focused on the victim of the first sacrifice rather than on sacrifice itself. It was to this first victim that the gratitude of the community was addressed, and it was the victim, rather than sacrifice itself, who was first divinized. This is how things happen in most archaic systems.

And this is also how things happen in the first and best known of all the books of the Vedas, the Rig Veda. The most celebrated text in this book is, I think, a type of founding myth entirely devoted to this first victim, in whom is incarnated the divine power of sacrifice. The victim is named Purusha. We will see further on that there exists in the Brahmanas a second founding myth of sacrifice, and it is not the victim this time who is divinized, but sacrifice itself, sacrificial activity. With respect to mimetic theory, this second myth is more perspicacious and altogether more interesting than the first but, for the moment, it is of the divinized victim in the much-celebrated *Hymn to Purusha* that I shall speak.

Hymn to Purusha

The text to which I refer is number 90 in the tenth and final book of the Rig Veda. Today the word purusha means simply, "man." In the hymn in question, it designates the first of all the sacrificial victims, someone impossible to define as a man in the usual sense of the term. The textbooks on mythology often define Purusha as a "primordial giant," and they place the text that we shall read in a subcategory of myths characterized by the central roles these giants play. There is one of them in China, another in Scandinavia. The Mesopotamian myth of Tiamat slain by Marduk figures frequently in this list.

The definition of Purusha as a type of primordial giant does not, however, correspond to the subject of the hymn. Purusha is gigantic, to be sure, and even more than gigantic, but he no more resembles what we understand by "giant" than what we understand by man. Here is the first strophe of the hymn:

> The Man has a thousand heads, a thousand eyes, a thousand feet. He pervaded the earth on all sides and extended beyond it as far as ten fingers.[12]

Purusha suggests something like a double of reality as a whole; he is a creation avant la lettre, containing the multitude of beings in a form that remains poorly differentiated. It is from this still formless form that the universe will emerge, by virtue of the first sacrifice:

> They anointed the Man, the sacrifice born at the beginning, upon the sacred grass. With him the gods, Sādhyas, and sages sacrificed.[13]

The fact that all the sacrificers preexist the first, original creation is not explained, any more than their number, which is, by all evidence, great. It is all the gods together, all the sages together, and also the seers, all the seers together, who immolate Purusha. Why are there so many of them? In an affair that appears as subdued and well ordered as this sacrifice, where does such a mob come from? We might readily conceive of Purusha as an enormous envelope bursting with reality, like a piñata that is struck during a festival, spilling the various gifts with which it is filled.

However suggestive it may be, my last image is not quite satisfactory, for Purusha is neither envelope nor container.

He is himself the agglutinated matter of all things, and the sacrificial act of creation consists in dismembering him, pulling him into pieces, into strips. Looking at Purusha, I think at once of the Dionysian sacrifice, of the terrible diasparagmos, the blind stampede of a hysterical mob against a victim, attacking with blows, with kicks, biting, and scratching, literally ripping him apart, tearing him to shreds. Only later are the assailants glorified with the title "sacrificers."

Certainly the two are not unalike, but the solemn tone and majestic serenity of the hymn contradict the hysterical fury of the Dionysian mania. The sacrifice of Purusha is anything but frenetic and improvised. It is presented as an action long and carefully premeditated, assured of its justice and legitimacy. We have the impression of a direct and positive response to a religious exigency deliberately confronted by a people too wise to evade it:

> From that sacrifice in which everything was offered,
> the melted fat was collected, and he made it into those
> beasts who live in the air, in the forest, and in villages.
> From that sacrifice . . . the verses and chants were

born, the metres were born from it, and from it the li-
turgical formulas were born.

Horses were born from it, and those other animals
that have two rows of teeth; cows were born from it,
and from it goats and sheep were born.

When they dismembered Purusha, into how many
parts did they apportion him? What do they call his
mouth, his two arms and thighs and feet?[14]

In this last strophe, the word "dismember" makes my ears prick
up. It raises again the suspicion I just dismissed. "Dismember"
brings to mind the Dionysian once again, and the final result
of a collective assault on the victim.

The sacrifice of Purusha might be the highly modified and
muted version of a scene that at first more closely resembled
the lynching of Pentheus by the Bacchantes than the hymn of
the Rig Veda. The tendency to minimize and even suppress
violence is at work always and everywhere in the rites, and
only an attentive examination can discover the traces of what
Durkheim called the "volcanic origin of the religious."

Mimetic theory is a radicalized Durkheimianism that, far
from moving in the direction of the rite, that is to say, its

effacement of violence, seeks instead to return to the violence, and quite deliberately takes the myth the wrong way. It seeks to make the violence it divines behind the myths reappear, even when the violence is considerably effaced as in the case of Purusha.

All the strips of Purusha, all the scraps of his flesh, are transformed into beings perfectly formed and constituted. Creative lynching remains highly visible in many religious systems, as distant from each other in time and space as pre-Socratic Greece from Aboriginal Australia at the end of the nineteenth century.

The bits and pieces torn from Purusha become the diverse components of the social order. Here now is the response of the hymn to the question that ends the preceding quotation:

> His mouth became the Brahmin; his arms were made into the Warrior, his thighs the Artisan; and from his feet the Servants were born.[15]

The diminishingly noble pieces of Purusha furnish the substance of the four "varnas"[16] in their hierarchical order: first the priests, then the warriors, then the artisans, and finally the outcasts. The original dismemberment is presented as a force of separation and spacing that produces not just living beings but the social divisions, the gods themselves, and finally the entire creation:

> Of Purusha is born the creative energy and the creative energy is born of Purusha. But only the sacrificers, by their violence, can liberate this energy and engender nature, the stars, the sun, the moon, the sky, the earth, the diverse animals, and likewise the religious hymns, the liturgy, the music, absolutely everything. The moon is born of his consciousness; of his gaze is born the sun; of his mouth Indra and Agni; of his breath is born the wind. The ethereal domain went out from his navel, from his head the sky, from his feet the earth, from his ear the East: thus were the worlds settled.[17]

The Vedic scriptures define creation in a rather "structuralist" fashion, in terms of spatial differentiation. The process is not a simple separation as in Lévi-Strauss; it is a sacrificial quartering. The role of sacrifice in the founding process is what structuralism refuses to see and it is this, too, that the rite, as it ages, vainly attempts to dissimulate—the fact that order should be generated by a paroxysm of disordered violence.

Everything that suggests the collective fury, everything that subtly contradicts the ritual serenity of our text seems to me a vestige, a trace of what is actually produced at the origin. This original lynching is effaced by innumerable repetitions that always reinforce the ritual effect par excellence: the conjuring away of violence, including here, finally, that of sacrifice itself, the negation of sacrifice.

In identifying the divine with the sacrificial victim, the *Hymn to Purusha* remains close to most archaic religions. Only the last strophe sounds a different note:

> The gods sacrificed the sacrifice by the sacrifice. Such
> were the first institutions. These powers had access to
> the firmament, where the Saints are, the original gods.[18]

In this last strophe, Purusha appears not only as the first victim—the passive face of sacrifice—but he assumes its other face, the sacrificial act itself. The two aspects are inseparable. This conclusion announces an idea that the Brahmanas will develop—the divinization of sacrifice in its active as well as passive forms.

Among the themes that should figure in the Hymn to Purusha but do not is the mythic accusation against Purusha, the fantastic and stereotypical accusation that mobilizes lynchers against an individual chosen by mimeticism, the accusation that justifies this choice and becomes unanimous despite its arbitrary character, the accusation that justifies the lynching in the eyes of the lynchers and that figures explicitly in most founding myths, in all accounts of scapegoat phenomena given by the persecutors.

There must have existed ancient versions of the *Hymn to Purusha* that made him a culprit, a parricidal and incestuous son, for example, in the style of the Greek Oedipus. This accusation must have been effaced with time, and this effacement itself inscribed in the general course of evolution toward the "religiously correct," which sooner or later characterizes any enduring culture.

Let us not forget it is the lynchers who tell us the origin of their sacrificial cult, and it is their error about the victim that makes him a "scapegoat." Even if, in the end, the founding victim passes for a savior, it always appears at first as though he must be killed because he is criminal, execrable, infinitely dreadful; otherwise, the agreement to kill him would never be reached, and his death would not reconcile the community. He would not therefore be divinized either. It is necessary that the victim first appear to "merit" his punishment, that he may later "merit" his divinity.

The communities do not notice, of course, the purely mimetic and mechanical nature of their religious experience. Since the victim is deemed the cause of the community's sufferings, it is the victim also, they think, who must have put an end to these sufferings. This is why, I repeat, he appears all-powerful, divine.

The genesis of myth is always a group of persecutors who transform their scapegoat, at first perceived as purely malevolent, into a benevolent divinity because of his reconciling power. To satisfy me entirely, and to verify mimetic theory, the *Hymn to Purusha* would need to contain a few more traces of the scapegoat mechanism in operation, in the form of a false yet indispensable accusation against the victim, which, unfortunately, is no longer present in the example that occupies us.

The Crime That Is Not There

This point is essential, and I shall therefore make it once more: sometime in an indeterminate past there must have been a crime attributed to Purusha. It was of course only a projection—imaginary but necessary for the fabrication of a really odious scapegoat. If Purusha no longer appears guilty, it must be due to the effects of time, which have effaced everything that in the genesis of the religious order is unsettling, anything that might potentially reveal the founding violence.

Purusha is irreproachable in the eyes of those who tear him to pieces. Why, then, would they tear him to pieces? The transcendental dimension of the myth is supposed to replace the real motive that has vanished, but this is only a late rearrangement of the facts, an effect of ritual wear and tear and the leveling down of all violence. The mythic accusation falls by the wayside, and all that remains in old and exhausted systems is veneration of the divinized victim. The religious impulse always evolves toward less violence and savagery, that is to say, toward what we have here. This is, moreover, proof of its effectiveness.

Because of this fairly typical evolution, the *Hymn to Purusha* lacks even indirect information about its own mythic structuration, about the scapegoat mechanism that necessarily produces it; nothing specific announces it apart from the details I pointed out at the beginning—the astonishing number of sacrificers and the dismemberment in which they are caught up.

All of this poses no problem in principle, but as a pedagogue I regret treating a myth so old and exhausted as this one, for I am deprived of the striking illustration I seek. It diminishes the demonstrative force of my thesis. To show that sacrifice emerges from a scapegoat phenomenon, I need a myth more robust than that of Purusha, who is not criminal enough for my taste. Neither the least little parricide nor the least little incest is attributed to him. The most spectacular feature of my demonstration hides itself the moment I need it.

Fortunately for me, there is something other than Purusha. There is a second founding myth of sacrifice in the Vedas, as I indicated a short while ago, and I shall turn to it now. The accusation we vainly seek in the *Hymn to Purusha* we shall find in the texts of the Brahmanas on Prajâpati, texts that are likely an amended and enriched reprise of the hymn.

Prajâpati

We turn back therefore to the Brahmanas and to that mythic creation I mentioned yesterday: Prajâpati. The myth is already a bit artificial, but extraordinary in its perspicacity. We shall later consult Prajâpati's criminal record—there exist several variants in the Brahmanas—and we shall have the satisfaction of finding there all we have sought in vain in the case of Purusha.

Sylvain Lévi urges us not to see Prajâpati as a god of sacrifice.[19] Such gods give us an impression of the divine and the sacrificial as two separate entities that join themselves for reasons that are fortuitous and alien to their respective essences. The union of the two is consubstantial and it is why Lévi calls Prajâpati the sacrifice god. I want to go even further in the same direction and call him the god sacrifice.

The word *prajâpati* literally means "lord of the creatures," and one finds it already in the Rig Veda, not far from the *Hymn to Purusha*. Why do the Brahmanas take up the word *prajâpati* rather than *purusha*? The two concepts are certainly close, but they are far from identical. That of the Brahmanas, probably the more recent, is more traditional than that which is in principle more ancient, and the tradition of the Brahmanas may well be the deliberate restoration of a crime that, because it is unanimously attributed to the god by his scandalized followers, justifies the primordial sacrifice. It is the crime in the name of which the entire community is mobilized against the scapegoat, who, by virtue of this fact, becomes a unifying and saving force. It is not necessary, I repeat, that he be truly culpable, but he must have appeared so in the eyes of his lynchers, the true authors of the myth, for it would not exist at all if they had not believed in the malevolence of their victim, the very one who would become their protecting divinity.

Modern anthropology has never unraveled this Gordian knot and it will not unravel it so long as it fails to understand that the accusation is real, that it bears upon a real victim, about whom we know nothing, of course, but whose reality is attested by the frequency of the same accusations in mob phenomena today. Crimes like parricide, incest, bestiality, and other analogous motifs are no doubt without objective foundation, but this does not make them any less real as accusations. Even today we find them in acts of collective violence—the witch hunt, for example. But these are always only aborted myths, in my judgment. Our skepticism, itself the product of an intellectual and spiritual evolution, prevents them from fully developing.

Not to interpret what the persecutors say as a real accusation, to see there, as we do today, a dream, poetry, fiction, "ludic activity," or other unreal things foreign to persecution, is to take them for fools; it is to re-mythify and think like persecutors, who take their own violence for something legitimate or at least negligible. Thus, the whole of myth is projected into the realm of the imagination, and this is how moderns are rid of their own violence, how they conjure away once more the scapegoat mechanism that for this reason continues to secretly structure their interpretations. It is the Freudian teaching on Oedipus, for example, which, far from demystifying the mythic accusations, absolutizes parricide and incest by attributing them to all men without exception.

The modern form of self-delusion is to take myth for something entirely imaginary, to make it pure fiction. The belief that myth is unrelated to any real phenomenon, that it has "purely symbolic" value, is as false as its inverse—faith in the literal veracity of the whole. In both cases, we fail to interpret in similar ways the mechanism that structures myth, the scapegoat phenomenon that we must take seriously without being taken in by it.

Myth is neither entirely fictive nor entirely real; it transfigures a phenomenon that the author-persecutors do not understand. Mimetic theory recovers the miserable truth. Myth is the work of persecutors who, having been reconciled at so little expense, are too complacent to show a critical spirit and rehabilitate their victim. Better to divinize him.

The Brahmanas charge Prajâpati with the very crime whose absence from the *Hymn to Purusha* I find so regrettable from a theoretical point of view, a crime ready-made to justify a lynching in the eyes of an archaic or backward mob: incest. Like Oedipus, like all divinities, Prajâpati's crime is not without extenuating circumstances, but they are not the same as those of Sophocles's hero. The god cannot become sexually active without making himself guilty of incest, since he is the father of all creatures without exception. When he makes love to the goddess Aurore, his daughter, all the other creatures are shocked and decide—unanimously, of course—to put him to death. It is the unanimity of the first lynching. The collective dimension is here, but the execution of the sentence is entrusted to a single god, the most cruel and sinister of Vedic gods, Rudra. Here is what Sylvain Lévi has to say:

> Prajâpati is unable to mate without committing incest. The Brahmanas are pleased to recount the crime of their God with customary indifference: "Prajâpati, it is said, wished to possess his own daughter—which would be Dyaus or good Usas (the sky or the dawn).—I want to mate with her, he said, and he possessed her. The gods considered this a crime: It is he, they thought to themselves, who treats his daughter, our sister thus. The gods said to the god who reigns over the beasts:

In truth, he commits a transgression, he who treats his daughter, our sister thus; let us pierce him. Rudra took aim at him and pierced him. . . . When the wrath of the gods dissipated, they healed Prajâpati and removed the spear from him." The details vary from text to text; the daughter of Prajâpati, for example, turns herself into a doe to escape the criminal passion of her father; he immediately changes himself into a stag. The Kausataki, which is often distinguished by a moral tendency, does not dare suppress the traditional incest, but transfers it from Prajâpati to his sons.[20]

Lévi finds the incest rather disturbing. He admits its traditional character, while failing to see its structural necessity. It is not out of respect for the tradition that the authors of the Brahmanas take up the accusation we found wanting in the Hymn to Purusha; it is because they divine its importance. Perhaps they found in their texts the incest we were unable to find; perhaps they have simply reinvented it. The ingenuity of their solution makes me think the second hypothesis is the correct one.

The fact that Prajâpati is deemed guilty and must suffer the punishment of the guilty does not prevent the Brahmanas from seeing in him the great creator god. Immediately after his execution his children pardon his crime and decide to resuscitate him. In other texts of the Brahmanas, there is neither incest nor punishment, but Prajâpati passes through the ordeal of death and resurrection all the same. It is his sacrificial activity that drains him and kills him. He collapses and falls in pieces, into the arms of his children—the gods who here, too, revive him and permit him to continue his work. The sacrifice god is submitted to the law of death and resurrection as its incarnation.

The authors of the Brahmanas are the unrivalled specialists of sacrifice. We must not conclude from all we read here that they demystify the myths in the same way that mimetic theory does. This demystification will eventually take place, but later, I think, at the end of the properly Vedic period, in the radically critical reflection on sacrifice in Buddhism, obviously, and in the Upanishads, of which I shall speak again tomorrow.

The disequilibrium, the mental confusion brought about by the mimetic crisis, facilitates sacrificial substitution, making it easier for members of the community to replace their mimetic rivals with the one destined to become a unanimous scapegoat. A certain drunkenness, therefore, a certain vertigo, is favorable to the success of sacrifice.

The authors of the Brahmanas have an intuitive sense for its conditions of possibility, for everything that facilitates the scapegoat mechanism. They know that sacrifice requires a loss of vigilance and lucidity if it is to produce the reconciling effect. This is indicated by the frequent recourse to hallucinogenic drugs and other means of reproducing the original frenzy, the perceptual havoc that facilitates sacrificial substitutions.

I spoke yesterday of the sacrificial beverage named soma. If scholars think it caused intoxication, it is because certain texts appear to support this hypothesis, and because trance-inducing procedures are widely used in sacrificial systems: participants smoke hemp, tobacco, etc; others spin round and round; yet others favor sexual excitation. These practices make the sacrificial substitutions more difficult for participants to see. The essential thing in sacrifice is to take one victim for another. Anything that diminishes the acuity of perception favors the success of sacrifice.

So let us return to the god Soma. The act of preparing the beverage is conceived as a sacrifice. But one cannot actually kill the god, since he is immortal. The act of sacrificing him, whatever its exact significance, is nevertheless a disagreeable, irritating experience for him. By sacrificing the god one is exposed to his reprisals.

Among the many individuals involved in preparing the sacred draught, the most imperiled were evidently those who crushed the stems of the soma to extract its sap, those properly called the sacrificers. What can be done to attenuate the danger? The texts suggest several highly revealing maneuvers. One advises the sacrificer to divert his attention from the god he is crushing, to think not of him but of someone else he would prefer to sacrifice if he had the choice. And the text here shows a revealing genius, probably involuntary but all the more striking if so:

When he deals the deathblow to Soma, he thinks of his
enemy; in the absence of an enemy he aims his thoughts
at a blade of grass.[21]

There is here, by all evidence, a full and complete revelation of the real function of sacrifice. It is no ordinary
sacrifice, to be sure, but the sacrifice of a god. What the
text recommends to the sacrificer to protect him from his
victim is to think expressly of the one whom he truly
desires to kill, the one whom he would perhaps kill if it
were not forbidden.

Because the sacrificial victim is here deemed even more
precious than the being for whom it is substituted, the ordinary sense of the substitution is inverted; by articulating this
inversion the text reveals the real function of sacrifice. It is a
strategy for preventing enemies from killing each other by
furnishing them with alternative victims. Nothing could be
more astonishing than the revelation of this game, which is
made possible by the cleverly maintained illusion that the violence perpetrated against the god is the more real and more
fearsome of the two. During this charade the truth appears

suddenly, a flash of lightning in the sky of sacrifice before the night covers it in darkness once more.

The text confirms our essential intuition. Sacrifice is a strategy for preventing violence from spreading throughout the community, for diverting toward an expendable victim the dangerous disorder that the murder of a personal enemy would precipitate, were it allowed. Sacrifice is an attempt to outwit the desire for violence by pretending, as far as possible, that the more dangerous and therefore more fascinating victim is the one being sacrificed rather than the enemy with whom we are obsessed in everyday life. The ancient Brahmins understood that, between the violence of men and that of sacrifice, a rapport exists that is no less essential for being concealed, and the text explicitly formulates this truth. Of all the sacrificial reflections on sacrifice, this one, I think, is the most revealing of all.

The scapegoat mechanism is the mechanism of substitution made utterly convincing by its unanimity so long as its mimetic nature goes unnoticed. We can easily demonstrate its presence not just at the heart of Vedic sacrifice, but on its periphery, notably in the sacrifice of the god Soma.

The risks the sacrificers run in the sacrifice of Soma begin, if we are to believe the Brahmanas, with the purchase of the plant from those who gathered it on the slopes of the Himalayas. The Brahmanas recommend that sacrificers explain carefully to the god that they are purchasing it solely for legitimate, even praiseworthy religious reasons:

> When one purchases soma, one purchases it to reign
> over the hymns, to dominate the hymns. In reality, one
> kills soma when one presses it; and so one says to it:
> I purchase you to reign over the hymns, to dominate
> the hymns, and not to put you to death.[22]

Buying or selling the god constituted an act so reprehensible that to divert his wrath it is not enough to lavish excuses and other protestations of virtue. The sacrificers resort to a stratagem characteristic of the Vedic sacrificial mentality. To divert the attention of the god, they strive to direct it toward a second-rate victim, a stranger, a vagabond. They propose to the god, in short, a false culprit, an insignificant scapegoat in place of those responsible, the actual sacrificers.

We have here a substitute victim in the most literal sense. The sacrificers offer the god a phantom buyer to make him forget the true buyers and consumers of his substance:

> Before using the soma, the priest presents the sacred stems to a person of the lower class, who then sells them to him at a high price. "Whoever sells the soma is wicked." He (this intermediary) is the villain in this drama, and it is on him that the wrath of the god and the punishment for the murder must fall.[23]

The idea of the scapegoat in the modern sense corresponds perfectly to the maneuver described here. If we fail to see it in the present case, we shall see it nowhere. We find in these texts two beliefs that make sacrifice possible but that appear to us incompatible. There is first the belief in the efficacy of substitutions, even the most deliberate, the most calculated. There is next the idea that the sacrificers can hide from the god the maneuver intended to deceive him. Perhaps they count on his passive complicity; perhaps they hope he will pretend to see nothing.

The sacrificers do not see, apparently, that their ignorance of the mechanism of victimization is what makes it effective. Or, in other words, they identify this mechanism, they understand it perfectly, and they continue nevertheless to ignore it because they believe in its protective virtue and are devoted to the game.

Ritual knowledge is practical, technical; it does not perfectly coincide with our present understanding, for we are unable to discover the scapegoat mechanism except by demystifying it as unjust and morally indefensible. We see it, consequently, as an ineffective means of negotiating with the divine unless the role of scapegoat is voluntarily assumed.

How can one hope to conceal from a god, who is supposed to read the human conscience like an open book, a dissimulation as crude as this? Perhaps one expects him to close his eyes, to make himself a passive accomplice in the maneuver. The ritual attitude depends here on a mélange of naïve credulity and extreme cynicism, though we do not see how they can coexist. To understand what obliges us to refuse, at least in principle, this manipulation of scapegoats, we must turn, I think, to the Judeo-Christian Scriptures, and this we shall do tomorrow.

3
Sacrifice Revealed in the Biblical and Vedic Religions

In my first two lectures, I found in the Brahmanas the phenomenon of the scapegoat, which is the basis for my theory of sacrifice. The phenomenon is sparked when mimetic rivalries reach their paroxysm and fasten suddenly on a single victim. The unanimous execration and destruction of a pseudo-enemy reconciles the community at the relatively modest cost of a single victim. The phenomenon is all the more valuable insofar as communities succeed in reproducing it using substitute victims: this is ritual sacrifice.

We find it everywhere and in forms too nearly alike to justify the theory that it is a pure fiction, a pseudo-institution. Modern anthropology embraces this error and so remains blind to the sacrificial and religious origins of humanity. Sacrifice is the primordial institution of human culture. It is rooted in mimeticism, a phenomenon far more intense in humans than in even highly mimetic animals. It is consequently more conflictual. The dominance patterns that constitute animal societies cannot be stabilized among humans. Mimetic crises arise and are resolved by scapegoat phenomena and their ritual repetitions. It must be in this way that specifically human societies commence: they are founded on sacrifices and the institutions derived from them.

Seeing that they are reconciled by their scapegoats but not quite sure why, the sacrificers mimic the founding violence as closely as possible. This is why sacrifice is completely universal, and universally recognizable. The actual sacrifices are, however, never perfectly identical. The founding event varies from one culture to another, within narrow limits, but it is never perfectly identical twice in a row. What also vary are the recollections of it and the interpretations to which it is submitted.

Sacrifices differ, but not so much as to justify the present relativism, the negation of all universality, and contempt for religion. Far from being simply "neurotic," the iron will to exactitude in imitation corresponds to a legitimate concern for efficacy. The domains of human activity most liable to generate conflicts—death, sexual relations, property, etc.—are those most regulated by sacrifices. All cultural institutions must be interpreted in terms of the transformations sacrifices undergo and the evolution that specializes them, little by little, into funerals, marriage, rites of initiation, schools, political power, etc.

The communities saved in extremis by their scapegoats are naturally incapable of recognizing, in the extraordinary violence that protects them, a pure and simple mimetic escalation of the ordinary violence that menaces them. This initial stage is purely naturalistic, materialistic even. And yet, mimetic theory never disdains human beings by attributing primitive religion to idiotic superstition like current anthropology does. It demonstrates why all archaic societies believe in the beneficial intervention of a supernatural power who teaches them their sacrifices. This supernatural power is generally assimilated to the first victim, the scapegoat.

By divining that the heart of the mystery is sacrifice itself, Vedic religion demonstrates an exceptional perspicacity. The Brahmanas appear bizarre only because of the incredible modern ignorance of religion. The Vedas go a long way in their understanding of sacrifice, but without escaping, in the texts we have read so far, the source of primordial error that characterizes archaic religion: the sacralization of reconciling violence.

Resemblances between Myths and the Gospels

But what of the Biblical and the Christian in the context of mimetic theory? If we reread the Gospels, we find there with little trouble the sequence of events common to founding myths and to the stories we have recounted from the Brahmanas. Here, too, a mimetic crisis precedes a scapegoat phenomenon.

Even those researchers most eager to reduce religion to an imaginary phenomenon are unable to deny, for once, that they are faced with something real. The crisis the Gospels describe, the gradual suffocation of the tiny Jewish state by Roman power, is doubtless historical. The majority of historians are furthermore agreed that Jesus really existed and that he died by crucifixion. At the paroxysm of the crisis, in the Gospels as in myths, a drama is set in motion that qualifies as "sacrificial" in the broad sense—the killing of Jesus. He is accused, like Oedipus, like all mythic heroes, of an unpardonable crime: he takes himself to be God. He will therefore be crucified and, in the end, he is divinized.

Why these resemblances?

During the first centuries of its existence, Christianity stirred up adversaries—Celsus, for example—who called attention to the facts I have just mentioned. There is in the Gospels a series of phenomena recalling the sequence of events in many earlier cults. Celsus made early use of these resemblances to contest the Christian claim of singularity. The Middle Ages interrupt the little game of comparisons that recommences in modern times, provoking such an interest that academics made it an independent discipline—the comparative study of religion, which has no interest, ultimately, but to demonstrate the banality of the Gospels in the context of world religion.

The Individual and the Mob in the Crucifixion

Christians follow these efforts anxiously, for they believe themselves vulnerable, evidently, to denials of the ultimate originality of their religion. Their mistrust of comparativism extends to mimetic theory as well. Although it shares neither the methods nor the mentality of the old comparative religion, mimetic theory compares the archaic and the Christian. This suffices to stir up mistrust, something the obvious results of my work are unable to dispel. What mimetic theory shows is that the singularity of Christianity is literally demonstrable, but on a paradoxical basis: the admission of all the resemblances so well observed, albeit naïvely, by the adversaries of this religion.

If we examine the accounts of the death of Jesus in light of mimetic theory, we see that mimeticism plays a major role among the passive witnesses, as it does among those who actively participate in the essentially collective violence of the crucifixion. The mimeticism appears foremost in the mob and in the imitation of the mob to which all the spectators of the crucifixion surrender. The tragic and caricatural example of this imitation is that of the bandits crucified to the right and left of Jesus (there is just one according to Luke). The fact that they are being crucified does not keep them from joining the mob by imitating them. The mob rails against Jesus, and so from their crosses the bandits rail, too. They have the illusion of belonging to this mob, of being men like the others. Pilate has nothing in common with these unfortunates, to be sure, but in the end he behaves just as they do: he does as the mob demands; he obeys them. To avoid the riot he dreads, he hands Jesus over. All the differences melt into mimetic unanimity. The mob is constituted and nourished by swallowing up everything that passes within its reach. It is the black hole of violent mimeticism; where mimeticism is most dense, the mob emerges.

The major example is that of Peter's denial: immersed in a mob hostile to Jesus, Peter cannot help but imitate their hostility. If we psychologize this denial, if we attribute it to the suggestible temperament of the apostle, we seek to prove (unconsciously) that in Peter's place, we would not have denied Jesus. It should be recalled that before his denial Peter, too, vows never to deny Jesus. He is too preoccupied with the opinion others have of him not to blindly adopt the politically correct attitude of the milieu at the center of which he has the misfortune of finding himself.

The mob that cries, "Crucify him!" had four days earlier welcomed Jesus as a conqueror. This reversal is a mimetic phenomenon so banal, so commonplace that the Gospels do not even acknowledge it. It is already present in the story of Job. His community has grown weary, it seems, of venerating its idol, and takes it into its head to lynch him.

It is mimeticism that summons all those who take part in the crucifixion, as actors or merely as spectators. It is mimeticism that makes Jesus what he quite evidently becomes at that moment, a *scapegoat* in the precise sense I have given this expression. The extreme solitude of Jesus is the other face of the anthropology of the scapegoat. It is so absolute that the victim has the impression of being rejected by God himself: "My God, my God, why hast thou forsaken me?"[24]

The perfection of the scapegoat is the unanimity of the mob, and it is to this that Peter alludes at the beginning of the Acts of the Apostles when he cites Psalm 2: "The kings of the earth set themselves in array, and the rulers were gathered together, against the Lord and against his Anointed."[25] In the third Gospel, which is also the work of Luke, Jesus appears not only before the high priest and Pilate, but before Herod, a third "king of the earth" who is also in Jerusalem. In order that there would be unanimity Herod must be given at least a small place, and this is what Luke does.

Luke deciphers the workings of mimeticism admirably. He takes the prophecies quite seriously, and with good reason, for the hostile mimeticism of mobs is something to which the Old Testament often alludes, to which its prophets are always falling victim (Jesus himself announces that he will die "like the prophets"). He is therefore not content adding Herod to the list of iniquitous judges before whom Jesus must appear, but mentions the cathartic effect of his participation in the abuse of the scapegoat: "And Herod and Pilate became friends with each other that very day, for before this they had been at enmity with each other."[26] Mimetic theory reveals the *mimetic* pertinence of certain Biblical citations that accompany the crucifixion in the Gospels, or in the Acts of the Apostles, those that tell of a great number of assailants gathering against a single victim, for example, or those that, in the Gospel of John, denounce the absurdity of unanimous violence: "They hated me without reason."[27]

The Presumed Identity of All Religions

All the actors and witnesses of the crucifixion are already hostile to Jesus or they become so, for mimeticism spares no one. Mimeticism is essential to myths as well, but it has to be deduced from indirect clues, and its action must be surmised. In the Gospels it is manifest, brilliant.

What I say appears to move in the same direction as the efforts of those who insist on resemblances between the Gospels and myths with the aim of denying the singularity of Christianity. Mimetic theory seems to crown these efforts by placing its finger on the cause of these resemblances, violent mimeticism. If the scapegoat is important when it remains dissimulated, it must be more important still when it is displayed in broad daylight, when it draws attention to itself. In the accounts of the Passion, instead of being hidden it is laid bare; it dominates everything.

This conclusion appears inevitable, but in reality it is not; it is even completely false. We are forced to the opposite conclusion, and for a very simple reason: the scapegoat cannot appear as scapegoat, as it does in the Gospels, without losing all credibility. To account for it, let us look more closely at an expression I have used throughout these lectures as if it signified something quite obvious—*scapegoat*. It is not an ordinary concept. Instead it is something paradoxical, a principle of illusion whose efficacy requires complete ignorance of it. To have a scapegoat is not to know that one has one. As soon as the scapegoat is revealed and named as such, it loses its power.

To reveal its purely mimetic nature, as the Gospels do, is to understand that there is nothing in the scapegoat phenomenon intellectually or spiritually deserving of faith; it is to see that the persecutors of any scapegoat, and not only of Jesus, hate him *without reason,* by virtue of an illusion that propagates itself irresistibly but no less unreasonably among them. It is pure, collective illusion, spectacular but deceiving. We cannot understand that the Gospels demystify this illusion without at once seeing that myths do not, and this powerlessness to demystify its own scapegoats fully defines archaic religion. Myths always present as truthful the patently absurd accusations to which Oedipus and a thousand mythic heroes are subject.

That Oedipus is guilty of parricide, I am prepared to believe; that he is guilty of incest is at least plausible; but that he is guilty of both crimes at once is simply incredible. And yet that is what myth affirms with the greatest seriousness. Every myth maintains that its single victim, its scapegoat, is in fact guilty; each ratifies the accusation that justifies the lynching and if the victim is later divinized, he remains above all the culprit of the preceding phase. Oedipus's whole "personality" reduces to his parricide and incest. Myths endlessly reflect the undemystified mimetic spiral. It is the single "thought" of the mob, to which is later added the gratitude of the lynchers, appeased by their own lynching. They attribute this appeasement to the victim and divinize him without ever discovering the miscarriage of justice of which they are guilty. The jury indulges the divinized hero, granting him some "extenuating circumstances," but nothing more, and the myth remains essentially a mendacious justification of collective violence.

Oedipus remains defined by his double crime, today more than ever. By making this hero the symbol of the human condition, Freud does no more than rejuvenate and universalize the eternal lie of mythology.

Instead of representing unanimous violence from the point of view of the deluded mob, the account of the crucifixion shows it for what it truly is. It makes visible the mimetic contagion and the inanity of the accusation. This is what emerges from our reading of the crucifixion. The Biblical accounts are the true representation of what in myths appears only in a misleading form dominated by the illusion of the lynchers. All such dramas result from the blindness of lynchers who incite one another against their victim.

Historically, the emergence of this truth begins well before the Gospels in the Hebrew Bible, which already rehabilitates a fair number of scapegoats, scapegoats who have been unjustly persecuted and expelled, if not always massacred. Joseph is an excellent example; Job is another. The narrators of the Psalms are often scapegoats who are about to be lynched and, like Job, they voice their anguish before the mob slowly closing in on them.

This is the true difference between the mythical and the Biblical. The mythical remains to the end the dupe of scapegoat phenomena. The Biblical exposes the lie by revealing the innocence of victims. If we fail to see the gulf that separates them, it is because, under the influence of the old positivism, we imagine that to truly differ texts must speak of different things. In reality, they differ radically because the Biblical breaks for the first time with the cultural lie par excellence, something never before revealed: the scapegoat phenomena on which human culture is founded. If the modern spirit marches over this abyss without even noticing it, it is because it has voluntarily fallen for the lie. We must not conclude that the abyss is not there.

The recounted event is essential since it is social injustice par excellence, but the manner of its representation is more essential still. In myths, there is but a single perspective on the scapegoat, that of the mob entirely mobilized against its victim, a mob that speaks with one voice. The victim, I repeat, appears justly condemned. Oedipus deserves his expulsion. In the Gospels, this perspective remains present, but it is discredited. It is still the perspective of the mob, the perspective of the greatest number, but it is no longer unanimous. It is victoriously denied by a small dissident minority who, after nearly succumbing to the collective contagion, rehabilitate the scapegoat. As precariously situated and meager as this small minority may be, it is the authentic voice of Christianity. It will be repressed, smothered, but never entirely eliminated. The future belongs to it and it will soon discredit all mythology forever.

The small evangelic minority will not only show men the absolute innocence of Jesus, that exceptional victim, it will show them the relative innocence, the irrelevance, of all history's scapegoats. This voice, even poorly understood, even deformed, ruins forever the credibility of mythic religions and sets in motion the greatest cultural revolution in history. Wherever the Gospels take root, sacrifices weaken and die out; archaic religion cannot reemerge.

To understand the difference between the mythical and the evangelic we must first accept and assimilate the resemblances, which do not render the two types of texts equivalent, as is still claimed today, but form the condition sine qua non of their essential divergence. It is always a scapegoat phenomenon that the great religious texts recount. But mythic religions recount it as if it were true, whereas the Biblical religion recognizes its falsity, despite extraordinary obstacles to this recognition. These obstacles arise from the fact that all the actors and spectators of the violence are convinced of its legitimacy. There are only false witnesses. Either the mimetic phenomenon occurs but is undetectable because unanimous, or it is not unanimous and so does not occur.

Nothing could be more mysterious therefore than the existence of texts that introduce truth in a world that is in principle closed to it. This truth has a religious dimension, but in a sense altogether different from that of myths. The divinity of Jesus is altogether different from that of mythic heroes, but it is also an anthropological and properly scientific truth. In their accounts of the crucifixion these texts provide us a rigorous deciphering of the mythological enigma indecipherable everywhere else.

Myths are never merely falsified accounts of mimetic escalations, but they are nevertheless misleading. The generative role of these escalations, once perceived, is confirmed indirectly in a number of ways: the fact, for example, that the single victim is everywhere and always believed to be more violent, more dangerous than the mob that is the true source of violence; or the fact that the victim is often endowed with signs that make him a preferential target for persecutors and predators, who are often attracted by physical marks that distinguish those who have them from an undifferentiated mob.

A founding myth is a scapegoat phenomenon deformed in a specific fashion and always recognizable because it is recounted by the lynchers themselves, the beneficiaries of the unanimous lynching who are always misled by the reconciliation it produces. The great Biblical dramas and the Gospels are scapegoat phenomena as well, but recounted this time by a minority who break away from the mob to denounce the mimetic escalation and rehabilitate the falsely accused victims.

It is the same phenomenal sequence in each case, the same mimetic escalation, the same scapegoat phenomenon, but in myths it structures the whole of the text because it structures the vision of their authors, the lynchers themselves. In the Gospels, it structures nothing; it is described with a wealth of impressive detail but it has become an inert theme in the text. It no longer misleads anyone.

The gathering against single victims requires a structuring power that can never fully exert itself except by concealing itself from the eyes of those whose vision it structures. It is a power of illusion to which archaic societies succumb, and consequently they know nothing of it. They are indebted to this power for their religious institutions, but they are unaware of its existence. Myths remain wedded to the mimetic illusion that rallies mobs against their victims and this is why they represent unanimous violence as the just punishment of culprits. It is also why they represent the first scapegoats as founders of sacrificial systems.

Instead of showing us, as myths do, a single victim who is always guilty, massacred by a mob that is always innocent, the Biblical texts and crucifixion accounts set right a truth always inverted by myths, one that, prior to the Biblical revelation, is found nowhere in the city of man. This is why the Gospels describe the human world as the kingdom of Satan, the Accuser, the one who has innocent victims condemned.

If the great religious texts were not all speaking of the same phenomenon, the same scapegoat mechanism, if they spoke merely of this and that, they would differ, to be sure, but their differences would hold neither religious nor anthropological interest. This would be the indifferent and fastidious difference of contemporary differentialism, the difference without identity of ideological neo-Saussureanism and other nonsense that contemporary nihilism embraces so as to conjure away all real problems, all truly interesting questions.

Judaism and Christianity are radically different from myths because they alone reveal a phenomenon whose existence myths do not even suspect, not because they are unfamiliar with it but because they are one with it. The Biblical and evangelic slowly deprive humanity of its last sacrificial crutches; they confront us with our own violence.

The Paradox of the Scapegoat

To understand that the scapegoat, far from being guilty, is innocent and arbitrarily chosen, is to destroy its structuring power; it is to truly demythify myths, or deconstruct them, if you like; it is to shatter archaic religion, but only the archaic. A religion is revealed that is entirely other and yet inseparable from the old.

We must therefore recognize the existence of a paradox in two parts. No text structured by a scapegoat phenomenon can reveal the mechanism that structures it. This first part of the paradox defines mythology. The second is Biblical: no text that reveals the scapegoat mechanism can be structured by it; it declares the truth of myth. The fact that this double paradox goes generally unnoticed by Christians themselves says much about the extraordinary affinity of the human race for scapegoats and about the nearly infinite resources of our hypocrisy for holding the Judeo-Christian revelation in check.

Nietzsche's colossal error was not to have seen what the unconscious nature of the scapegoat phenomenon implies for the relation between the mythic and the Biblical. It is sacrificial religions that embody slavery in all its forms, whereas the Biblical and Christian attain a truth and freedom that humans may put to very bad use, certainly, but that frees them from mythological domination forever.

They are completely deceived, who accuse the Gospels and the Bible of thinking in terms of scapegoats and covert persecutions because they speak openly of these things whereas myths never speak of them. Myths never speak of them because they are entirely possessed by them. They are completely deceived, who hold that myths are too luminous, too sunlit, too Greek to be guilty of secret persecutions.

They Know Not What They Do

The proof that the Gospels see what myths do not—the unconscious dimension of scapegoat phenomena—is their attitude vis-à-vis the murderers of Jesus, which is without vengeance, contrary to what we are told today. Far from mercilessly stigmatizing these unfortunates, the Gospels see in them men like others; they did what men have always done and still do today under analogous circumstances.

The crucifixion is unique in its theological aspect, but terribly banal from an anthropological point of view. The essential phrase here is that of Jesus during the crucifixion: "Forgive them, Father, for they know not what they do."[28] In Acts, Peter makes plain in his discourse to the crowd at Jerusalem that we are to take these words literally. He explains to these men that neither they nor their leaders—who are even more culpable—need despair at the extent of their crime. There is no question here of effacing the guilt of the murderers but of affirming it as a consequence of a properly universal ignorance.[29] The fact that the victim is the only son of God does not make the murderers more culpable than other men. Not to see this is to miss the essence of the Christian revelation.

The Gospels Know What They Do

Yet another thing confirms the mimetic interpretation: its explicit presence in the Gospels. Only the Gospels are truly capable of summarizing the observations we have just made about the crucifixion. All that we have observed is admirably formulated and reformulated in the Gospel texts themselves; in the titles, for example, that his companions confer upon Jesus or that Jesus confers upon himself. They each describe, in a metaphorical but transparent way, an extremely violent form of what I have called the scapegoat mechanism.

One phrase that makes the phenomenon in question explicit is that pronounced by the high priest Caiaphas justifying the plot against Jesus: "It is expedient for you that one man should die for the people, and that the whole nation should not perish."[30] Thanks to just one victim a great number is saved. It is the definition I have myself given of sacrifice.

Another expression that defines the foundational role of the scapegoat is found in Psalm 118: "The very stone which the builders rejected has become the head of the corner."[31] Jesus asks his hearers to explain this phrase but no one responds. It obviously has to do with the single victim, the universally expelled scapegoat who in the end is discovered at the summit of the religious edifice founded by him and upon him. It is what will happen to Jesus: the form of the process is the same, only its signification is different.

To all the titles of Jesus in the synoptic Gospels, we must add the definition of the logos in the Gospel of John. Those who try to minimize the originality of the Christian Logos by insisting on the Greek origin of this notion fail to see that the Johannine definition has nothing to do with the Greek. It incorporates the essential Christian idea of the exclusion, the expulsion, to that of the Logos, so as to define a scape-Logos, if I dare say, something altogether foreign to Greek thought:

> The light shines in the darkness,
>
> And the darkness has not overcome it. . . .
>
> He was in the world,
>
> And the world was made through him,
>
> Yet the world knew him not.
>
> He came to his own home,
>
> And his own people received him not.[32]

The light has shone in the darkness, and the darkness has rejected it. All of this is found as well in other, longer texts—the parables for example, and that of the wicked vinedressers in particular, the most extraordinary of all from our perspective. It shows that the unanimous mob and the murder of Jesus are preceded by a long series of analogous phenomena, all interpreted as violent attempts to completely dispossess the master, God the Father, of his vineyard, by mistreating each of his messengers and lastly his own Son, who is assassinated. The homicidal vinedressers turn all God's envoys into scapegoats.

One might object that the word "scapegoat" never appears in the Gospels, and to this I respond that the word itself is of little importance; all that matters is the reality behind it. There exists, moreover, in the New Testament, an expression applied to Jesus alone that captures everything the word "scapegoat" signifies; the metaphor is very close to the one I use but far superior to it. The expression is "lamb of God," which rids us of the pointless vulgarity of the goat and makes even more visible the innocence of the unjustly sacrificed victim.

Moderns who see in the Gospels a myth of death and resurrection like the others reach this conclusion on the basis of real, observable analogies, but these hardly suffice to abolish all differences between the mythic and the Christian. To truly apprehend this relation, we must begin by admitting the resemblances in question, by seeing that, as in myths, the Gospels report a scapegoat phenomenon; unlike myths, however, which reflect the mechanism of unanimity without ever understanding it, the Gospels reveal this same mechanism and, to the extent this revelation is assimilated, render it incapable of functioning. Wherever the Gospels take root, blood sacrifices disappear forever.

Return to the Brahmanas

What I have just said about the Bible and the Gospels comes close to declaring the absolute superiority of the Judaic and Christian over other religions, and notably over the Vedic tradition. All we have heard about the latter indicates a rigorous, often subtle thought, but one that remains within the sacrificial framework and is always interpreted in mythic fashion. It is rooted in scapegoat phenomena that remain undeciphered and inseparable from the sacrificial illusion.

Actually our general survey is too limited to justify any conclusion. We will not have time to complete our study, but I cannot conclude these lectures without mentioning certain developments essential to our theme, even if we are unable to treat them at greater length. They have to do, of course—my audience suspects it—with the presence of an anti-sacrificial and even nonsacrificial inspiration in the most advanced parts of the Vedic tradition, those which announce the great Indian mysticism of the Upanishads, as well as those which, leaving India, ultimately give rise to Buddhism.

I have neither the time nor competence sufficient to wade into all of this, but I shall nevertheless cite two texts that bear directly upon sacrifice and attest to a great change with respect to it. My first text is found in the book that provided the better part of my first two lectures, *La Doctrine du sacrifice dans les Brahmanas,* by Sylvain Lévi. The only one of its kind in Lévi's collection, it is presented as a satirical, even boldly comic fable directed against traditional, sacrificial piety. The slightly ridiculous hero of this text is the primordial man, Manu. He is always represented as a model of piety, and that is the case here as well. His piety consists above all in always accepting the Brahmins' offer to sacrifice for him, in his name.

What suggests satire is that the sacrificers have only selfish motives for proposing to their clients sacrifices so onerous that they are transformed into calamities, sacrifices that deprive their clients of what is necessary, indispensable. The sacrificers here are associated with the Asuras, selfish and malicious demons who care only about their own comfort:

> Exclusively occupied with the effects of sacrifice,
> Manu shows the same indifference to the gods as to
> the Asuras; they are in his eyes no more than effective
> agents that set in motion the all-powerful mechanism.
> With an even and imperturbable *sang-froid,* he cedes to
> the divine and demonic sacrificers his utensils, his bull,
> his own wife, and even his guests, confident in the ne-
> cessity of the anticipated outcome.

Manu had some vessels; if they clattered, all the Asuras who heard the clatter ceased to exist that day. Now, there were in those days among the Asuras two Brahmins, Trstra and Varutri; they said to the two: Cure us of this evil. The two Brahmins said: Manu, you are a sacrificer; faith is your god. Give us these vessels. He gave them to them; they destroyed them by means of fire. A bull licked the flames; the voice entered into him. If it bellowed, all the Asuras who heard it bellowing ceased to exist that day. Trstra and Varutri said: Manu, you are a sacrificer; faith is your god; we will sacrifice this bull for you. They sacrificed the bull for him; the voice passed into the wife of Manu; if she spoke, all the Asuras who heard it ceased to exist that day. Trstra and Varutri said: Manu, you are a sacrificer; faith is your god; we will sacrifice your wife for you. They splashed her with water, led her around the fire, and prepared the wood and the grass.

Indra observed: These two hypocrites among the Asuras deprive Manu of his wife. Passing himself off as a Brahmin, Indra approached and said, "Manu, you are a sacrificer; faith is your god. I want to sacrifice for you."

"Who are you?"

"A Brahmin. What is the use of asking after the father of a Brahmin or his mother? If you can find in him the sacred science, that is his father, that is his grandfather."

"What will be the offering?"

"These two Brahmins."

"Am I the lord of these two Brahmins?"

"You are their lord; whosoever offers hospitality is the lord of his guests. He advanced to destroy the second altar. [The false Brahmins] brought the wood and the grass; they said [to Indra]: What are you doing there?"

"I am sacrificing for Manu."

"With what?"

"With you. They knew then that it was Indra; they threw down the wood and the grass and ran away. . . . Manu said to Indra: Complete my sacrifice, that my sacrifice not be lost. He said to him: What you desire by sacrificing her you will have; but leave this woman. And he let his wife go."[33]

Behind the demons the entire caste of Brahmins is visible. The Brahmins' role in sacrifice was one of passive surveillance, but of the honorarium paid by the sacrificers they took the lion's share. The account is therefore a scathing satire of the way the religious "establishment" exploits the piety of sacrificers.

Manu accepts sacrifices that are more and more disastrous for his household and himself. It is a sacrificial escalation that we see: the false Brahmins first sacrifice Manu's bowls, which is to say his material possessions, precious no doubt in the eyes of a man who has almost nothing, but of little objective value. Next comes the bull, more valuable than the bowls, clearly, but less so than the third victim, a human being this time, and none other than Manu's own wife. Manu's excessive respect toward sacrifices and the sacrificers leads to increasingly catastrophic renunciations, until the moment when the great god Indra interrupts the game and alerts the sacrificers that they risk becoming victims in their turn. Blind obedience to the sacrificial imperative recommended by the crafty Brahmins leads Manu toward an abominable murder until Indra intervenes to pull him from the clutches of the two demons.

This ironic critique of sacrifice recalls that of certain prophets of Israel and in particular a text from Micah that traces the same sacrificial escalation in order to condemn its self-destructive tendency. The human sacrifice here is that of the first-born son, a practice long prevalent in the Middle East that Judaism had abolished, but which had a tendency to persist outside the law.

To restore to sacrifice an efficacy it has lost, its most pious devotees tend to raise the stakes, offering victims ever more precious without seeing the danger of this practice, its regressive and finally self-destructive character:

> With what shall I come before the Lord,
> And bow myself before God on high?
> Shall I come before him with burnt offerings,
> With calves a year old?
> Will the Lord be pleased with thousands of rams,
> With ten thousands of rivers of oil?
> Shall I give my first-born for my transgression,
> The fruit of my body for the sin of my soul?[34]

When sacrifice seeks to recover its efficacy by selecting ever more precious victims, it turns against the very beings it should protect; it regresses toward human victims. It loses all coherence. Sacrifice is preserved only by further aggravating the religious crisis caused by its growing inefficacy. In the end the two texts, the Vedic and the Biblical, formulate the same critique of sacrifice, which pretends to divert men from violence but actually encourages it. There is the same understanding on both sides, but in India it is expressed in an ironic and satirical fashion.

To conclude I will cite another satire of Vedic sacrifice that is not unrelated to the two preceding texts. It is borrowed from a collection entitled the Buddha Birth Stories, and it seems to me very close in spirit to the account of Manu and his sacrifices. Here again, sacrifice is diverted from its first use, but this time the king's sacrificer makes a deliberately selfish and criminal use of the power it possesses:

Once upon a time, when Brahmandatta reigned in Benares his chaplain was tawny and had lost all his teeth. This chaplain's wife was carrying on an intrigue with another Brahman of like physique. Since he could not break it, he resolved to destroy his rival, so he went to the king and told him the southern gate of his city was ill put together (that is, without the correct rites) and was unlucky: it must be pulled down, and a new one built of lucky timber after making a sacrifice under an auspicious constellation to the spirits that guarded the city; the victim must be a tawny toothless Brahman of pure blood on both sides. The king agreed, but the fool could not refrain from boasting of it to his wife. She warned her man, who escaped after spreading the news, so that all those who had the same peculiarities fled the city. Being the only one left who fulfilled the conditions, the king's chaplain was seized for execution.[35]

This text reminds me of another, the Oedipus Rex of Sophocles, and of the meditation that Hölderlin devoted to it a little while before he lost his mind. Hölderlin wonders whether Oedipus, by interpreting the oracle "too infinitely," that is to say by reading in it a demand for criminal investigation, does not call down upon himself the reprisals of Creon, who succeeds in making Oedipus the "scapegoat" that Oedipus wanted to make of Creon. One often falls into the trap he lays for his adversary. This could well be the lesson of Oedipus Rex; it is certainly the lesson of the two sacrificial accounts that I read you earlier. The one who thinks to take is himself taken. I leave you with this idea. . . .

Notes

1. Henri Hubert and Marcel Mauss, "Essai sur la nature et la fonction du sacrifice," in Marcel Mauss, *Œuvres* (Paris: Éditions de Minuit, 1968), 1: 193–354; English trans.: Henri Hubert and Marcel Mauss, *Sacrifice: Its Nature and Function,* trans. W. D. Halls (Chicago: University of Chicago, 1964).

2. Joseph de Maistre, "Traité sur les sacrifices," in *Les Soirées de Saint-Pétersbourg* (Paris: Librairie Garnier Frères, 1888); English trans.: Joseph de Maistre, "Elucidation on Sacrifices," in *St. Petersburg Dialogues,* trans. Richard A. Lebrun (Montreal: McGill-Queen's University Press, 1993).

3. René Girard, *La Violence et le sacré* (Paris: Grasset, 1972); English trans.: René Girard, *Violence and the Sacred,* trans. Patrick Gregory (Baltimore: Johns Hopkins, 1977).

4. Sylvain Lévi, *La Doctrine du sacrifice dans les Brahmanas* (Paris: PUF, 1966).

5. Henri Hubert and Marcel Mauss, "Essai sur la nature et la fonction du sacrifice," vol. 1.

6. Lévi, *La Doctrine du sacrifice dans les Brahmanas,* 48.

7. Lévi, *La Doctrine du sacrifice dans les Brahmanas,* 51.

8. Lévi, *La Doctrine du sacrifice dans les Brahmanas,* 44.

9. Lévi, *La Doctrine du sacrifice dans les Brahmanas,* 36. The presence of mimetic desire in the Brahmanas strikes me as all the more certain in light of one further account paraphrased and commented upon by Sylvain Lévi. It attracts our attention by what separates it from the other accounts, and this difference is easy to define: a feminine being plays the essential role, which does not happen very often in the Brahmanas. The dramatic process that unfolds in this text does not lead to sacrifice and actual physical violence plays no part. We might therefore think that it has little in common with the furious rivalries of the gods and demons, and yet we find desire and mimetic rivalry once again, for the comportment of the female character is dominated by coquetry and nothing is more mimetic than coquetry.

The only difference is that coquetry and the episode that portrays it are situated in the upper, still benign regions of mimetic desire, foreign to physical violence but governed by the same laws. It is a place where women play a part, a region of exclusively psychological violence. Even though this episode does not end in sacrifice, the desire in question is as mimetic as everywhere else.

The female character to whom I allude is centered on a word in the feminine gender. Vâc signifies the voice, speech, language. The Brahmanas treat the word and the thing in a manner that we could call allegorical. Allegorically, they make of it a woman, seductive but so vain that she believes herself superior to sacrifice itself. Her pretensions curiously recall those of recent and sensational theories that pretend to dissolve the real into language:

> The gods and the Asuras, both the issue of Prajâpati, possessed the heritage of Prajâpati their father . . . the gods possessed the sacrifice, Yajna, the Asuras possessed the voice, Vâc. . . . The gods said to Yajna: Vâc is woman; call out to her and she will surely bid you come. . . . He thought to himself: Vâc is woman; I will call out to her and she will bid me come. He called out to her. But at first she showed him only indifference. And this is why when called by a man, a woman shows only indifference at first. He said: From a distance she has shown me only indifference. They [the gods] said to him: Call out to her, lord, and she will surely bid you come. He called out to her. She did not speak to him so much as toss her head. And this is why, when a man calls to a woman, she does not speak to him but merely tosses her head. He said: She did not speak to me so much as toss her head. [The gods] said: Call out to her, lord, and she will surely bid you come.

He called out her and she bid him to come close to her. And this is why in the end a woman bids a man to come close to her. He said: She bid me to come close to her. The gods considered: Vāc is woman. Let her not draw him to her side [the side of the demons]! Speak to her in these words: I remain here, come to me—then, when she comes declare it to us. Therefore, as he remained in place, she came to him. And this is why, when a man remains in place, the woman comes to him. He declared her arrival to them: She is arrived, he said. Thus the gods parted her from the Asuras. (Lévi, *La Doctrine du sacrifice dans les Brahmanas,* 31–32)

For the Brahmanas, Vāc is of course beneath sacrifice but she is important nonetheless and the gods have an interest in luring her into their camp. But how to separate Vāc from the Asuras? The problem is all the more delicate as Vāc, good coquette that she is, is delighted to find herself courted at the same time by the Devas and the Asuras. She would like to prolong the situation indefinitely without ever choosing one of the two camps. Yajna forces her hand by resorting to the most classic maneuver of mimetic desire: he feigns indifference.

Coquetry is not rooted in the riches it parades but in poverty and nakedness. This impoverishment is contradicted by its speech but confirmed by its behavior. It falls everywhere into the crudest traps because it is ruled by a lack of being. Because the coquette secretly despises herself, indifference alone attracts her and she turns away from all whom she attracts. Sylvain Lévi calls Yajna's maneuver vulgar. This is a bit severe. The maneuver is ubiquitous because it is everywhere effective, in the East as well as in the West, and this text proves it. Mimetic desire is characteristic of no one culture because it is characteristic of all, beyond a certain level of leisure and refinement.

10. Lévi, *La Doctrine du sacrifice dans les Brahmanas,* 83.

11. Translators' footnote: The confusions to which Girard refers are elaborated in the third lecture.

12. Madelaine Biardeau and Charles Malamoud, *Le Sacrifice dans l'Inde ancienne* (Louvain-Paris: Peeters, 1996), 79: 14–15. Trans. note: While largely following the translation of the Hymn to Purusha, we have also consulted translations contained in: Wendy Doniger O'Flaherty, trans. and annotator, *The Rig Veda: An Anthology* (Harmondsworth: Penguin Books, 1981), 30–32, and Wm. Theodore de Bary, ed., *Sources of Indian Tradition* (New York: Columbia University Press, 1958).

13. Biardeau and Malamoud, *Le Sacrifice dans l'Inde ancienne,* 14–15.

14. Biardeau and Malamoud, *Le Sacrifice dans l'Inde ancienne*.

15. Biardeau and Malamoud, *Le Sacrifice dans l'Inde ancienne*.

16. All of the castes and their subdivisions belong to one of the four varnas, who supervise the entire system but have no real existence.

17. Biardeau and Malamoud, *Le Sacrifice dans l'Inde ancienne*, 14–15.

18. Ibid.. O'Flaherty notes (*The Rig Veda: An Anthology*, 32n18): "The meaning is that Purusha was both the victim that the gods sacrificed and the divinity to whom the sacrifice was dedicated; that is, he was both the subject and object of the sacrifice. Through a typical Vedic paradox, the sacrifice itself creates the sacrifice."

19. Lévi, *La Doctrine du sacrifice dans les Brahmanas*, 15–16.

20. Lévi, *La Doctrine du sacrifice dans les Brahmanas*, 20–21.

21. Lévi, *La Doctrine du sacrifice dans les Brahmanas*, 130n1.

22. Lévi, *La Doctrine du sacrifice dans les Brahmanas*, 170.

23. Lévi, *La Doctrine du sacrifice dans les Brahmanas*.

24. Mark 15:34; Biblical citations taken from the Revised Standard Version.

25. Psalm 2:1–2, cited in Acts 4:25–26.

26. Luke 23:12.

27. John 15:25; Psalm 35:19; Psalm 69:4.

28. Luke 23:34.

29. Acts 3:17.

30. John 11:50.

31. Psalm 118:22–23; Luke 20:17–18.

32. John 1:5–11.

33. Lévi, *La Doctrine du sacrifice dans les Brahmanas,* 118–20.

34. Micah 6:6–7.

35. Jataka, IV, 245 ff; quoted in A. M. Hocart, *Kings and Councillors* (Chicago: University of Chicago, 1970), 193.